5 YOUR -Minute JOURNAL

5 YOUR -Minute JOURNAL

Find Gratitude and De-stress with Simple Daily Exercises

Amy Birch

Illustrated by Emilie Anne Jenks

Michael O'Mara Books Limited

First published in Great Britain in 2022 by
Michael O'Mara Books Limited
9 Lion Yard
Tremadoc Road
London SW4 7NQ

A CIP catalogue record for this book is
available from the British Library.

Papers used by Michael O'Mara Books Limited are natural,
recyclable products made from wood grown in sustainable
forests. The manufacturing processes conform to the
environmental regulations of the country of origin.

ISBN: 978-1-78929-430-9 in paperback print format

1 2 3 4 5 6 7 8 9 10

Designed and typeset by Natasha Le Coultre and Claire Cater
Cover design by Natasha Le Coultre
Cover and internal illustrations by Emilie Anne Jenks

Printed and bound in China

www.mombooks.com

This journal belongs to:

_____

_____

Introduction

In a world that so often focuses our attention on what's going wrong or what we're told we lack, gratitude can be a simple and powerful antidote. It connects us with what we do have, here and now, while revealing fresh perspectives and overlooked sources of positivity. And it can give us a solid grounding in what really matters to us as we make decisions about how we'd like to move forward.

No wonder the benefits are so well documented. For example, practising gratitude on a regular basis helps build our sense of happiness, contentment, resilience, optimism and connection. It can change the way you see and feel about the world and yourself within it. It can even have an impact on your physical health, such as by aiding better sleep, lowering blood pressure and stress, and boosting the immune system. The key to all of this is the practice part, and that's why having a gratitude journal can be so useful. A few minutes every day is enough to start making a difference. Just make sure to give yourself enough time to really pause and give

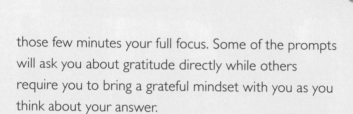

those few minutes your full focus. Some of the prompts will ask you about gratitude directly while others require you to bring a grateful mindset with you as you think about your answer.

You'll notice that each week has its own theme to help you explore your world in greater variety and depth, and at the end of each week there's space for noting down your reflections on what the experience has been like for you. Were some days easier to fill in than others? Did any of the prompts bring up important feelings or memories? Did you notice any changes to your mood across the week? Were there any surprises? There are also more in-depth 'Wellbeing Challenges' scattered throughout the book that will help you develop your gratitude practice by building self-awareness and self-compassion, as well as further supporting your wellbeing.

Start any day you like and see what a year of practising gratitude can do.

Begin at the Beginning

MON

A person you feel grateful for. _____

An object you feel grateful for. _____

An experience you feel grateful for. _____

TUES

Describe what gratitude feels like. _____

_____

WEDS

The first three things that come to mind when you think of gratitude.

1. _____

2. _____

3. _____

THURS

Something you felt grateful for ...

this morning. _____

this afternoon. _____

this evening. _____

Three ways you were able to meet your needs today.

1. _____

2. _____

3. _____

What three things are you most grateful for this week?

1. _____

2. _____

3. _____

Reflections

_____

_____

_____

_____

_____

The Seasons

MON

Three things you appreciate about spring.

1.

2.

3.

TUES

Three things you appreciate about summer.

1.

2.

3.

WEDS

Three things you appreciate about autumn.

1.

2.

3.

THURS

Three things you appreciate about winter.

1. _____

2. _____

3. _____

FRI

Describe the seasonal changes you feel most grateful for.

_____

_____

WEEKEND

What three things are you most grateful for this week?

1. _____

2. _____

3. _____

Reflections

_____

_____

Life's Soundtrack

MON

The loudest sound you can hear right now. _____

The quietest. _____

The most pleasant. _____

TUES

Your three favourite sounds.

    1. _____

    2. _____

    3. _____

WEDS

A sound that signals that ...

    something good is about to happen. _____

    there's something to be wary of. _____

    you can relax now. _____

THURS

The first sound you heard this morning. _____

The last one you'll likely hear tonight. _____

The best one you heard today. _____

Three sounds you can hear right now and what they're telling you.

1. _____

2. _____

3. _____

What three things are you most grateful for this week?

1. _____

2. _____

3. _____

Reflections

_____

_____

_____

_____

_____

Friends

MON

Three people who you feel lucky to have in your life.

1. _____

2. _____

3. _____

TUES

What do you particularly appreciate about the first person?

_____

_____

WEDS

How about the second person? _____

_____

_____

THURS

And the third? _____

_____

_____

FRI

Three things that make you a good friend.

1. _____
2. _____
3. _____

WEEKEND

What three things are you most grateful for this week?

1. _____
2. _____
3. _____

Reflections

_____

_____

_____

_____

_____

Family

MON

What does family mean to you? _____

_____

TUES

Three things you value most about your family (whoever that means to you).

1. _____

2. _____

3. _____

WEDS

When have your family ...

helped support you? _____

taught you something valuable? _____

surprised you? _____

THURS

How do you help support your family? _____

_____

FRI

Three family memories that make you smile.

1. _____

2. _____

3. _____

WEEKEND

What three things are you most grateful for this week?

1. _____

2. _____

3. _____

Reflections

_____

_____

_____

_____

_____

Your Wellbeing Challenge

Practising gratitude allows us to connect more consciously with the positives in our life, both within and without, which in turn can affect how we're feeling. By becoming more familiar with the full spectrum of our feelings, what influences them and how we experience them, we can recognize what else is helping or what else we might need. Try the following exercise when you notice a shift in your mood.

How do you feel right now? _____

_____

_____

_____

What do you think might be contributing to the way you're feeling?

_____

_____

_____

_____

Where in your body are you holding your feelings? For instance, excitement can feel like a fullness in the chest or anger can be held in the tightness of the jaw.

_____

_____

_____

_____

How would you like to respond to yourself when you're feeling like this? What advice would you give to a good friend?

_____

_____

_____

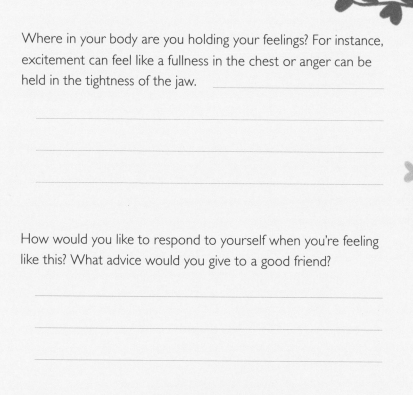

'WHEN EATING FRUIT, REMEMBER THE ONE WHO PLANTED THE TREE.'

Ralph Waldo Emerson

Past but Never Gone

MON Three things from your past that helped you navigate today.

    1. _____

    2. _____

    3. _____

TUES Three things from the past week that had a positive impact.

    1. _____

    2. _____

    3. _____

WEDS Three things from the past month that are still important today.

    1. _____

    2. _____

    3. _____

Three things from the past year that you don't want to forget.

1. _____

2. _____

3. _____

Three things from your childhood that you wouldn't change.

1. _____

2. _____

3. _____

What three things are you most grateful for this week?

1. _____

2. _____

3. _____

Reflections

_____

_____

And Relax

MON

Three places where you unwind.

1. _____

2. _____

3. _____

TUES

Your favourite ...

relaxing music. _____

soothing scent. _____

comfort food. _____

WEDS

Describe how it feels when you're fully relaxed. _____

_____

THURS

Your three favourite calming activities.

1. _____

2. _____

3. _____

FRI

Make a plan here to help you find a moment of calm today.

_____

_____

_____

WEEKEND

What three things are you most grateful for this week?

1. _____

2. _____

3. _____

Reflections

_____

_____

_____

_____

_____

Entertain Me

MON

Your favourite ...

    movie. _____

    TV show. _____

    book. _____

TUES

Three creators (writers, artists etc.) who you feel most grateful for.

    1. _____

    2. _____

    3. _____

WEDS

Your guilty pleasure. _____

What do you love about it? _____

THURS

The last time a book/movie/TV show/etc ...

    totally gripped you. _____

    brought you to tears. _____

    made you laugh until it hurt. _____

Give three friends a recommendation for something you think they'll enjoy.

    1. _____

    2. _____

    3. _____

What three things are you most grateful for this week?

    1. _____

    2. _____

    3. _____

Reflections

_____

_____

_____

_____

_____

Fully Charged

MON

Three ways you support your energy levels.

1. _____

2. _____

3. _____

TUES

Your favourite heart-pumping activity. _____

When was the last time you did it? _____

When could you do it next? _____

WEDS

Describe how your body and mind feel when your energy levels are high. _____

_____

THURS

Three ways you recharge your emotional batteries.

1. _____

2. _____

3. _____

FRI

Make a brief, achievable plan for how you could better
support your energy levels next week. _____

_____

_____

WEEKEND

What three things are you most grateful for this week?

1. _____

2. _____

3. _____

Reflections

_____

_____

_____

_____

_____

Favourite Places

MON Your top three places in the whole world.

1. _____

2. _____

3. _____

TUES What do you love about the first place? _____

How do you feel when you're there? _____

_____

WEDS And the second place? _____

How do you feel when you're there? _____

_____

THURS And the third place? _____

How do you feel when you're there? _____

_____

Where you go to enjoy the …

view. _____

atmosphere. _____

company. _____

What three things are you most grateful for this week?

1. _____

2. _____

3. _____

Reflections

_____

_____

_____

_____

_____

Your Wellbeing Challenge

Sometimes when we reflect deeply we can find ourselves confronting uncomfortable or distressing thoughts, memories or sensations. Having a go-to grounding technique means we can re-anchor ourselves to the safety and stability of the present. Try this simple grounding technique now to get a feel for it and then keep practising.

1. Sit in a comfortable chair with your feet flat on the floor. You can close your eyes if you like.

2. As you sit there allow your breathing to slow and deepen.

3. Next, notice your weight pressing into the seat of the chair and along the back rest. Notice the sensation of resistance as the chair holds you in place.

4. If the chair has arms, lay your own arms along them or place your hands on top. Notice any textures you can feel.

5. Move your attention to your feet on the ground. Wiggling your toes can help.

6. Push the soles of your feet gently into the ground.
   Notice how the ground pushes back to keep you steady.

7. Now, with your whole body held by the chair and the
   ground, bring your attention back to your breath as you
   inhale and exhale deeply for another minute or so.

8. When you're ready, open your eyes.
   No need to hurry getting up.

'GRATITUDE IS A DIVINE EMOTION: IT FILLS THE HEART, BUT NOT TO BURSTING; IT WARMS IT, BUT NOT TO FEVER.'

Charlotte Brontë

Sweet Anticipation

MON

Three things that you are looking forward to this week.

1. _____

2. _____

3. _____

TUES

Describe your strongest childhood memory of 'I just can't wait for ...'

_____

_____

_____

WEDS

What are you most looking forward to ...

in the coming month? _____

_____

in the coming year? _____

_____

even further into the future? _____

THURS

What time of year do you most look forward to? _____

What's special about it? _____

_____

FRI

Describe the sensation of anticipation in three words.

1. _____

2. _____

3. _____

WEEKEND

What three things are you most grateful for this week?

1. _____

2. _____

3. _____

Reflections

_____

_____

Challenges

MON

The three greatest challenges you've overcome.

1. _____

2. _____

3. _____

TUES

What helped you overcome the first challenge? _____

_____

WEDS

What about the second? _____

_____

THURS

And the third? _____

_____

FRI

A goal you set yourself that was tough but worth it. _____

_____

A risk that paid off. _____

Your next challenge. _____

WEEKEND

What three things are you most grateful for this week?

1. _____

2. _____

3. _____

Reflections

_____

_____

_____

_____

_____

Surprises

MON

What's positive about surprises (even if you don't enjoy them in general)? _____

_____

TUES

The three best surprises you've had.

1. _____

2. _____

3. _____

WEDS

A time when things worked out better than you expected.

_____

What had you predicted would happen? _____

What actually happened? _____

THURS

How have you surprised someone? _____

When have you surprised yourself? _____

_____

FRI

What happened today that you didn't expect? _____

_____

How did it turn out in the end? _____

_____

WEEKEND

What three things are you most grateful for this week?

1. _____

2. _____

3. _____

Reflections

_____

_____

_____

_____

_____

Wonder

MON

Three things that blow your mind (in a good way).

1. _____

2. _____

3. _____

TUES

When were you last awestruck? _____

_____

How would you describe the sensation? _____

WEDS

A massive thing that brings you a sense of wonder. _____

_____

A tiny thing. _____

An everyday thing. _____

Three things you can see right now that work/were made in a way you don't understand.

1. _____

2. _____

3. _____

An invention that brings you a sense of wonder. _____

A part of the natural world. _____

A part of you. _____

What three things are you most grateful for this week?

1. _____

2. _____

3. _____

Reflections

_____

_____

The Present

MON

One thing that you feel grateful for having now that you didn't have in the past. _____

What difference has it made to your life? _____

_____

_____

TUES

Something else that you didn't used to have. _____

What difference has it made to your life? _____

_____

WEDS

And another. _____

What difference has it made to your life? _____

_____

THURS

One more. _____

What difference has it made to your life? _____

_____

And lastly ... _____

What difference has it made to your life? _____

_____

What three things are you most grateful for this week?

1. _____

2. _____

3. _____

Reflections

_____

_____

_____

_____

_____

Your Wellbeing Challenge

Feed your gratitude practice by making more time for the good stuff. Sounds simple, but when was the last time you dedicated ample time to planning fun?

Fill this page with things that you enjoy doing. Think of things that make you laugh, give you a sense of purpose, of contentment, of exhilaration. Big and small, it all counts. When you're finished, start making plans to actually do them!

_____

_____

_____

_____

_____

_____

_____

_____

_____

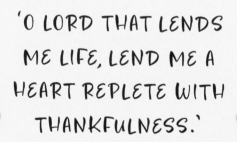

'O LORD THAT LENDS ME LIFE, LEND ME A HEART REPLETE WITH THANKFULNESS.'

William Shakespeare

Kindness

MON

Three times you have shown kindness to others.

1. _____

2. _____

3. _____

TUES

Describe how you feel after you have shown someone

else kindness. _____

_____

WEDS

Three acts of kindness that you have received.

1. _____

2. _____

3. _____

THURS

Describe how you feel after you have been on the

receiving end of kindness. _____

_____

How did you last show your gratitude for someone's kindness?

What act of kindness could you do today?

How could you show yourself kindness today?

What three things are you most grateful for this week?

1.

2.

3.

Reflections

Stories

MON

A story that ...

changed your mind about something. _____

helped you understand yourself better. _____

opened up a new world to you. _____

TUES

Your top three stories (from books, podcasts, conversations etc.).

1. _____

2. _____

3. _____

WEDS

The best true story you've ever heard. _____

What was special about it? _____

_____

THURS

If you were to write a story, what would it be about?

_____

FRI

Your favourite ...

story from childhood. _____

story to tell about yourself. _____

storyteller. _____

WEEKEND

What three things are you most grateful for this week?

1. _____

2. _____

3. _____

Reflections

_____

_____

_____

_____

_____

The Gratitude Awards

MON

Today's award for ...

    'Small Act of Kindness' goes to ——————————

    'Making You Smile' goes to ——————————

    'Being Dependable' goes to ——————————

TUES

The lifetime award for ...

    'Being There For You' goes to ——————————

    'Always Making You Laugh' goes to ——————————

    'Trustworthiness' goes to ——————————

WEDS

What three awards would you give today and to whom?

    1. ——————————

    2. ——————————

    3. ——————————

THURS

What awards might you have earned today?

_____

_____

FRI

As part of your acceptance speech, who do you want to thank?

_____

WEEKEND

What three things are you most grateful for this week?

1. _____

2. _____

3. _____

Reflections

_____

_____

_____

_____

Gifts

MON

Three gifts you have felt grateful for receiving.

1. _____

2. _____

3. _____

TUES

Three gifts you loved giving.

1. _____

2. _____

3. _____

WEDS

A precious gift you've received that was not an object. _____

_____

A gift you often give without realizing it. _____

_____

A gift you receive without realizing it. _____

_____

THURS

How do you feel when you give someone you care about a gift?

_____

How do you feel when you receive one? _____

FRI

What small gift could you offer yourself today? (It doesn't have to be a physical thing.) _____

And what could you offer someone else? _____

_____

WEEKEND

What three things are you most grateful for this week?

1. _____

2. _____

3. _____

Reflections

_____

_____

Come Rain or Shine

MON

Your three favourite types of weather.

1. _____

2. _____

3. _____

TUES

What do you appreciate about the first? _____

_____

_____

WEDS

And the second? _____

_____

_____

THURS

How about the third? _____

_____

_____

FRI

Three things that varied weather makes possible.

1. _____
2. _____
3. _____

WEEKEND

What three things are you most grateful for this week?

1. _____
2. _____
3. _____

Reflections

_____

_____

_____

_____

_____

Rest

MON

Three occasions when you have felt at peace.

1. _____

2. _____

3. _____

TUES

The best dream you ever had. _____

_____

_____

Your last daydream. _____

_____

WEDS

Describe how it feels when your mind is at rest. _____

_____

THURS

Describe how it feels when your body is at rest. _____

_____

_____

FRI

Three things that get better when you're well rested.

1. _____

2. _____

3. _____

WEEKEND

What three things are you most grateful for this week?

1. _____

2. _____

3. _____

Reflections

_____

_____

_____

_____

_____

Your Wellbeing Challenge

Lots of us have a mental filter, a sort of unconscious bias that only allows us to take in evidence that supports our current ideas about ourselves and others. Unfortunately, it often operates even when those theories have a negative impact. For instance, you might see yourself as not being very good at your job, and so you filter out any evidence that doesn't fit in with that idea. You might discount it, such as, 'Yeah, I got good feedback, but I bet everybody did, it doesn't mean anything.' Or you might just ignore it altogether. A lot of people don't even know they're doing it.

Practising gratitude is a good way of counteracting an over-active negative filter, in that it shuts off the autopilot and prompts us to consciously pay attention to what's going well for us. But we can all have our own personal filters, so keep an eye out this month for what you might not be letting in.

_____

_____

_____

_____

_____

'APPRECIATION IS
A WONDERFUL THING.
IT MAKES WHAT IS
EXCELLENT IN OTHERS
BELONG TO US
AS WELL.'

Voltaire

Cut Grass and Fresh Laundry

MON

Your three favourite scents.

1. _____

2. _____

3. _____

TUES

Describe a time when you felt grateful for your sense of smell.

_____

WEDS

Your favourite ...

cooking smell. _____

smell from nature. _____

smell in your home. _____

THURS

What smell is most evocative for you? _____

_____

What memories does it bring up? _____

_____

FRI

Three things you can detect with your nose right now.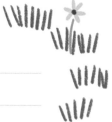

    1. _____

    2. _____

    3. _____

WEEKEND

What three things are you most grateful for this week?

    1. _____

    2. _____

    3. _____

Reflections

_____

_____

_____

_____

_____

The Very Basics

MON

Three things that you literally couldn't survive without.

1. _____

2. _____

3. _____

TUES

Do you have access to reliable shelter? _____

What might it be like not to? _____

_____

WEDS

Do you have access to sufficient food? _____

What might it be like not to? _____

_____

THURS

Are you able to keep yourself warm? _____

What might it be like not to? _____

_____

FRI

Describe a time when you felt grateful for being able to meet your basic needs. _____

_____

_____

WEEKEND

What three things are you most grateful for this week?

1. _____

2. _____

3. _____

Reflections

_____

_____

_____

_____

_____

Skills

MON

Three skills that you rely on.

1. _____

2. _____

3. _____

TUES

A skill you worked hard to obtain. _____

And one which came naturally. _____

A skill you have that would surprise your younger self. _____

_____

WEDS

What do you see as your most valuable skill? _____

How did you learn it? _____

_____

THURS

What skill are you most proud of? _____

And is there one that you're still developing? _____

_____

Three abilities that you take for granted.

1. _____

2. _____

3. _____

What three things are you most grateful for this week?

1. _____

2. _____

3. _____

Reflections

_____

_____

_____

_____

_____

Breaks and Holidays

MON

When and where were your three favourite holidays?

1. _____

2. _____

3. _____

TUES

Your favourite place to visit. _____

What do you love about it? _____

WEDS

When did you last take a proper break? _____

Where did you go? _____

What did you enjoy doing? _____

_____

THURS

When can you take your next break? _____

Where would you like to go? _____

What would you like to do? _____

_____

FRI

Three benefits you experience after a break.

1. _____
2. _____
3. _____

WEEKEND

What three things are you most grateful for this week?

1. _____
2. _____
3. _____

Reflections

_____
_____
_____
_____
_____

Me

MON How would a close friend describe you? _____

_____

TUES Three things about you that you wouldn't change.

1. _____

2. _____

3. _____

WEDS Describe a time when you have felt proud of yourself.

_____

_____

THURS Three ways that you can show yourself kindness.

1. _____

2. _____

3. _____

FRI

Thank your past self for something you did in the last ...

day. _____

week. _____

month. _____

WEEKEND

What three things are you most grateful for this week?

1. _____

2. _____

3. _____

Reflections

_____

_____

_____

_____

_____

Your Wellbeing Challenge

During the next few weeks, take some time to tune into how you treat yourself. Pay particular attention to when you're struggling or feel like you've made a mistake. How are you speaking to yourself? What words are you using? What tone? If a good friend came to you with the same problem, would you treat them in the same way? If you find that you're more critical than encouraging then you're certainly not alone. Many of us have learned to be harsh or punishing to ourselves. Sometimes it's so ingrained that it becomes automatic and we can forget that maybe that voice isn't speaking the truth.

Noticing when we're being unkind to ourselves is the first step. Pausing and offering ourselves the chance to do things differently is the next.

How could you imagine doing it differently?

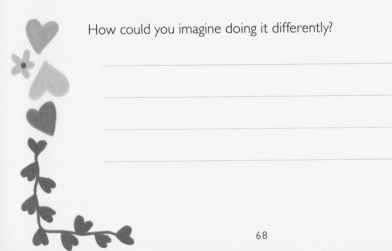

'DO NOT SPOIL WHAT
YOU HAVE BY DESIRING
WHAT YOU HAVE NOT;
REMEMBER THAT WHAT
YOU NOW HAVE WAS ONCE
AMONG THE THINGS YOU
ONLY HOPED FOR.'

Epicurus

Creativity

MON — Three things/people that inspire your creativity.

1. _____

2. _____

3. _____

TUES — Three ways you used your creativity today.

1. _____

2. _____

3 _____

WEDS — Three times you used your creativity without realizing it.

1. _____

2. _____

3. _____

THURS

Your favourite imaginary ...

childhood game. _____

happy place. _____

story. _____

FRI

The last time you thought creatively to overcome a challenge.

_____

The place where you feel most inspired. _____

WEEKEND

What three things are you most grateful for this week?

1. _____

2. _____

3. _____

Reflections

_____

_____

Home

MON

Three things you appreciate about your home.

1. _____

2. _____

3. _____

TUES

Where in your home do you feel ...

most comfortable? _____

most creative? _____

most connected? _____

WEDS

Three things about your home that are underappreciated.

1. _____

2. _____

3. _____

THURS

Where do you feel most at home? _____

What is it about that place that's special? _____

FRI

Your favourite room. _____

What do you like most about it? _____

_____

WEEKEND

What three things are you most grateful for this week?

1. _____

2. _____

3. _____

Reflections

_____

_____

_____

_____

_____

Your Neighbourhood

MON Three things you appreciate about your local area.

1. _____

2. _____

3. _____

TUES What changes in your neighbourhood do you feel grateful for?

_____

And what are you pleased has stayed the same? _____

_____

WEDS Your favourite local ...

story. _____

little-known gem. _____

event. _____

THURS How would you welcome a new neighbour to the area?

_____

If you were to move away, what would you miss the most?

1. _____

2. _____

3. _____

What three things are you most grateful for this week?

1. _____

2. _____

3. _____

Reflections

_____

_____

_____

_____

_____

The Best Things in Life are Free

MON

Three things that you feel grateful for that come for free.

1. _____

2. _____

3. _____

TUES

What do you particularly appreciate about the first? _____

_____

_____

WEDS

How about the second? _____

_____

_____

THURS

And the third? _____

_____

_____

FRI

Three things you can see right now that cost nothing and contribute to your life.

1. _____

2. _____

3. _____

WEEKEND

What three things are you most grateful for this week?

1. _____

2. _____

3. _____

Reflections

_____

_____

Behind the Scenes

MON From refuse collectors to farmers, shopworkers to healthcare professionals, who would you like to thank today?

1. _____

2. _____

3. _____

TUES Three people whose behind-the-scenes work helped you to eat today.

1. _____

2. _____

3. _____

WEDS Three people whose behind-the-scenes work helped you get to where you needed to go.

1. _____

2. _____

3. _____

THURS

Three people whose behind-the-scenes work mean you have a place to live.

    1. _____

    2. _____

    3. _____

FRI

Thank a stranger who contributed to your day. _____

_____

WEEKEND

What three things are you most grateful for this week?

    1. _____

    2. _____

    3. _____

Reflections

_____

_____

Your Wellbeing Challenge

When we practise gratitude we're consciously choosing to notice the positives in our life, and as a result we get to experience the warmth, sense of connection and optimism that that kindles. We can enjoy even more of those experiences by choosing to give our attention to other positives too. It can be as simple as asking yourself, what went well today? And, what part did I play in it? Remember to keep a curious and compassionate mindset, and to include all the little things. As well as directly countering negative filters, it's an effective way of slowly strengthening that encouraging internal voice.

Try it out for the coming week and jot down here what you notice. If you find it helpful you could keep it up longer-term. As with gratitude, it's regular practice that makes the difference.

Monday _____

_____

Tuesday _____

_____

Wednesday _____

_____

Thursday _____

_____

Friday _____

_____

Saturday _____

_____

Sunday _____

_____

Opportunity

MON

Three opportunities that you have embraced.

1. _____

2. _____

3. _____

TUES

What impact did the first one have on your life? _____

_____

_____

WEDS

How about the second one? _____

_____

_____

THURS

And the third? _____

_____

_____

FRI

Three opportunities you would like to pursue in the future.

1. _____

2. _____

3. _____

WEEKEND

What three things are you most grateful for this week?

1. _____

2. _____

3. _____

Reflections

_____

_____

_____

_____

_____

Work

MON

Three things (no matter how small) you achieved today.

1. _____

2. _____

3. _____

TUES

Your favourite job from the past. _____

What did you enjoy about it? _____

_____

WEDS

Three reasons you do the work (whatever that means) you do.

1. _____

2. _____

3. _____

THURS

Work you are most proud of. _____

What part of your work doesn't feel like 'work'? _____

_____

FRI

Three things you tend to underappreciate about working.

1. _____

2. _____

3. _____

WEEKEND

What three things are you most grateful for this week?

1. _____

2. _____

3. _____

Reflections

_____

_____

_____

_____

_____

Memories

Your three most treasured memories.

MON

1. _____

2. _____

3. _____

TUES

Your earliest happy memory. _____

What details can you remember? _____

_____

WEDS

Three ways you keep important memories close.

1. _____

2. _____

3. _____

THURS

A cherished keepsake. _____

What does it remind you of? _____

FRI

Who do you enjoy reminiscing with? _____

_____

A forgotten memory that you were grateful to be reminded of.

_____

_____

WEEKEND

What three things are you most grateful for this week?

1. _____

2. _____

3. _____

Reflections

_____

_____

Heroes

MON — Three people who you admire.

1. _____

2. _____

3. _____

TUES — What is it about the first person that you look up to? _____

_____

_____

WEDS — How about the second person? _____

_____

_____

THURS — And the third? _____

_____

_____

FRI

Three ways you inspire yourself.

1.
2.
3.

WEEKEND

What three things are you most grateful for this week?

1.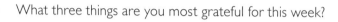
2.
3.

Reflections

_____

_____

_____

_____

_____

The Little Things

MON

The last thing you did ...

for fun. _____

to relax. _____

for someone else. _____

TUES

Three things (no matter how small) you do every day to support your body, mind or spirit.

1. _____

2. _____

3. _____

WEDS

What do you appreciate about ...

what you're wearing right now? _____

the last meal you had? _____

what you're doing right now? _____

THURS

What did you last ...

say thank you for? _____

accomplish (no matter how small)? _____

give yourself credit for? _____

FRI

Are there any other little things you'd like to give some appreciation to? _____

_____

WEEKEND

What three things are you most grateful for this week?

1. _____

2. _____

3. _____

Reflections

_____

_____

At Your Fingertips

MON

Three textures you enjoy.

1. _____

2. _____

3. _____

TUES

Your comfiest piece of clothing. _____

The softest thing you've ever stroked. _____

The best hug-giver. _____

WEDS

Three textures you can touch right now.

1. _____

2. _____

3. _____

THURS

Cool or cosy? _____

Smooth or textured? _____

Soft or sturdy? _____

What would make you feel more comfortable right now?

_____

_____

_____

What three things are you most grateful for this week?

1. _____

2. _____

3. _____

Reflections

_____

_____

_____

_____

_____

Your Wellbeing Challenge

There may be times when you don't want to practise gratitude or feel like things are so bad that there's nothing to be grateful for. It's important not to discount sadness or anger, or feel like we have to force ourselves to take a positive mindset. Experiencing and expressing our feelings is important. It's our way of processing what's happened to us. So if you need to give yourself a break to attend to how you're feeling then do it. At these times you might find the first Wellbeing Challenge in this book, about checking in with your feelings, useful as an alternative to your gratitude practice.

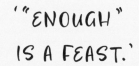

'"ENOUGH"
IS A FEAST.'

Buddhist proverb

Out and About

MON

Your favourite place to ...

    eat. _____

    shop. _____

    hang out. _____

TUES

Three things you were grateful for the last time you went out.

    1. _____

    2. _____

    3. _____

WEDS

Where you go to ...

    get close to nature. _____

    collect your thoughts. _____

    see something beautiful. _____

THURS

Where you like to go with friends. _____

Where you go to be alone. _____

FRI

Three things you enjoyed doing out of the house in the last week.

1. _____

2. _____

3. _____

WEEKEND

What three things are you most grateful for this week?

1. _____

2. _____

3. _____

Reflections

_____

_____

_____

_____

_____

Your Body

Three things you're grateful that your body can do.

MON

1. _____

2. _____

3. _____

Three skills you've taught your body.

TUES

1. _____

2. _____

3. _____

Three ways you care for your body.

WEDS

1. _____

2. _____

3. _____

THURS

Three things your body is doing for you right now.

1. _____

2. _____

3. _____

SOAP

SOAP

FRI

Three ways you could be kinder to your body.

1. _____

2. _____

3. _____

WEEKEND

What three things are you most grateful for this week?

1. _____

2. _____

3. _____

Reflections

_____

_____

The Music that Makes Us

MON

A song that ...

you can't help but sing along to. _____

always brings you to the dance floor. _____

has got you through a tough time. _____

TUES

The best live music event you've ever been to. _____

What was great about it? _____

_____

WEDS

A musician that has inspired you. _____

What do you admire about them? _____

_____

THURS

The musical sound you enjoy the most. _____

What do you love about it? _____

_____

FRI

What piece of music – album, concerto, whale song, whatever – would you like to give your time and attention to next week?

_____

_____

WEEKEND

What three things are you most grateful for this week?

1. _____

2. _____

3. _____

Reflections

_____

_____

_____

_____

_____

The Natural World

MON

Three things that you appreciate about the natural world.

1. _____

2. _____

3. _____

TUES

Your favourite ...

animal. _____

bird. _____

plant. _____

WEDS

Where do you encounter nature on a daily basis? _____

_____

What about these encounters do you feel most grateful for?

_____

_____

THURS What kind of natural environment do you enjoy being in most and how do you feel when you're there?

FRI Describe a memory of being in nature as a child.

WEEKEND What three things are you most grateful for this week?

1.

2.

3.

Reflections

The Future

MON Three things that are coming up in your future that you feel grateful for.

　　1. _____

　　2. _____

　　3. _____

TUES What makes you especially appreciate the first? _____

_____

_____

WEDS What about the second? _____

_____

_____

THURS And the third? _____

_____

_____

FRI

Make a short, achievable plan for bringing a touch more positivity to next week.

_____

_____

_____

WEEKEND

What three things are you most grateful for this week?

1. _____

2. _____

3. _____

Reflections

_____

_____

_____

_____

Choices

MON Three choices that changed the course of your life.

    1. _____

    2. _____

    3. _____

TUES Three choices that you were able to make today.

    1. _____

    2. _____

    3. _____

WEDS Three things that don't always feel like choices but are.

    1. _____

    2. _____

    3. _____

THURS

What is a choice in your past that you've struggled with, and how might you offer your past self some compassion?

_____

_____

FRI

What one thing could you do a little differently today, and what difference might it make? _____

_____

WEEKEND

What three things are you most grateful for this week?

1. _____

2. _____

3. _____

Reflections

_____

_____

Your Wellbeing Challenge

Mindfulness and meditation are brilliant for training your mind to stay in the moment, avoiding the pull to spin off into worries about the future or regrets about the past. They can help you live life as it happens. Try this mindful breathing exercise before you do your next gratitude practice and see what difference it makes. If you find it useful there are lots of videos online as well as websites, books and apps that can teach you how to take it further.

Sit in a comfortable position. Closing your eyes can also help you to focus.

Bring your attention to the air flowing into and out of your lungs. Notice how it feels as it passes in through your nose and down into your chest.

As you breathe out keep your attention on the flow of air and the changing sensations in your body.

Now start to take deeper, slower breaths. Bring the air down further into your lungs (as far as is comfortable).

Notice the sensations of your chest expanding and your diaphragm pulling down. You can place your hand on your belly so you can feel it rise and fall.

When your attention wanders, don't worry, it's all part of the process. Just notice this, too, and then gently guide your attention back to your breath.

Carry on for as long as is comfortable. You could start by aiming for a minute or two and then work up to five.

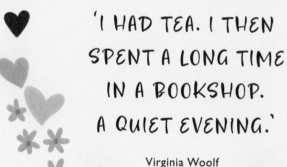

'I HAD TEA. I THEN SPENT A LONG TIME IN A BOOKSHOP. A QUIET EVENING.'

Virginia Woolf

Interests and Passions

MON

Your top three interests or passions.

1. _____

2. _____

3. _____

TUES

What do you love about the first? _____

_____

_____

WEDS

How about the second? _____

_____

_____

THURS

And the third? _____

_____

_____

FRI

Three topics from the past week that kindled your curiosity.

1. _____

2. _____

3. _____

WEEKEND

What three things are you most grateful for this week?

1. _____

2. _____

3. _____

Reflections

_____

_____

_____

_____

_____

Flavour-filled

MON Your three favourite foods of all time.

1. _____

2. _____

3. _____

TUES Favourite ice cream flavour. _____

Savoury or sweet? _____

Favourite cook. _____

WEDS The meal you most look forward to. _____

Your favourite food growing up. _____

Most memory-stirring taste. _____

THURS What did you appreciate the most about the last thing you ate?

_____

And the last thing you drank? _____

FRI

What would you include in your ideal three-course menu?

1. _____

2. _____

3. _____

WEEKEND

What three things are you most grateful for this week?

1. _____

2. _____

3. _____

Reflections

_____

_____

_____

_____

_____

Inventions and Discoveries

MON An invention that makes your life ...

easier. _____

more connected. _____

fun. _____

TUES Three developments in medicine that have benefitted you.

1. _____

2. _____

3. _____

WEDS A discovery that ...

caused you to make changes in your life. _____

blew your mind. _____

gives you hope for the future. _____

THURS If you could invent or discover one thing, what would it be and why?

_____

What three innovations would your younger self never have guessed?

1. _____

2. _____

3. _____

What three things are you most grateful for this week?

1. _____

2. _____

3. _____

Reflections

_____

_____

Motivation

MON

Describe how it feels when you're motivated. _____

_____

_____

TUES

Who empowers you? _____

Who do you empower? _____

WEDS

Three things that help you take action.

1. _____

2. _____

3. _____

THURS

Three things that keep you going.

1. _____

2. _____

3. _____

FRI

When has persistence paid off?

When has letting something go paid off?

WEEKEND

What three things are you most grateful for this week?

1.

2.

3.

Reflections

Wisdom

MON

A lesson you learned through experience.

What was important about it?

TUES

Another lesson.

What was important about it?

WEDS

And another.

What was important about it?

THURS

One more.

What was important about it?

FRI

And finally. _____

What was important about it? _____

_____

WEEKEND

What three things are you most grateful for this week?

1. _____

2. _____

3. _____

Reflections

_____

_____

_____

_____

_____

Freedoms

MON

What words best describe the feeling of freedom?

_____

TUES

The last three choices that you were able to exercise.

1. _____

2. _____

3. _____

WEDS

What 'freedom from ...' are you most grateful for?

_____

What 'freedom to ...' are you most grateful for?

_____

THURS

Three freedoms that you have now that your parents didn't.

1. _____

2. _____

3. _____

FRI

How do you remind yourself of your own power to make changes? _____

_____

Who can you rely on to help you do that? _____

_____

WEEKEND

What three things are you most grateful for this week?

1. _____

2. _____

3. _____

Reflections

_____

_____

Your Wellbeing Challenge

Making changes and choices, and generally taking ownership of our lives, can be a tricky business. It means getting to know what we really want and our personal priorities, then turning that knowledge into action. It can mean upsetting our sense of others' expectations while accepting that by taking one path we are letting go of other options. No wonder we sometimes avoid decisions or struggle to feel empowered.

See if you can connect with your own priorities and power as you consider these questions.

Is there something that you would like to be different?

_____

_____

_____

What might it look like if it were different?

_____

_____

_____

What would help you make a small step in that direction?

_____

_____

What might the next step be after that?   _____

_____

_____

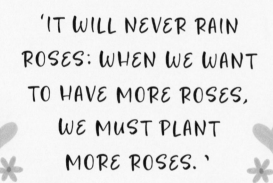

'IT WILL NEVER RAIN
ROSES: WHEN WE WANT
TO HAVE MORE ROSES,
WE MUST PLANT
MORE ROSES.'

George Eliot

Values

MON Three values you'd like to live your life by.

1. _____

2. _____

3. _____

TUES Describe how you incorporate the first value into your life.

_____

_____

WEDS And the second value. _____

_____

_____

THURS And the third. _____

_____

_____

FRI

Describe how, in the future, you could align your choices even further with your values. _____

_____

_____

WEEKEND

What three things are you most grateful for this week?

1. _____

2. _____

3. _____

Reflections

_____

_____

_____

_____

_____

Pass it On

MON

Three ways you could express your gratitude this week.

1. _____

2. _____

3. _____

TUES

Three acts of kindness you could do this week.

1. _____

2. _____

3. _____

WEDS

When did you say thank you today? _____

What else could you have expressed gratitude for? _____

_____

THURS

Is there a big gesture of appreciation that you'd like to plan for the coming year? _____

_____

FRI

What new and creative ways could you use to express gratitude?

1. _____

2. _____

3. _____

WEEKEND

What three things are you most grateful for this week?

1. _____

2. _____

3. _____

Reflections

_____

_____

_____

_____

_____

Amy Birch grew up in Oxford before studying at the University of Cambridge where she received a BA (Hons) in History. Since then, she has pursued careers in publishing and psychotherapy. She is a professional counsellor and is a registered member of the BACP (British Association for Counselling and Psychotherapy). She enjoys gardening and crafts in her spare time.

Emilie Anne Jenks is an illustrator and maker specializing in wall art, home decor, greetings cards and hand-painted ornaments. She lives in the land of endless prairies and cotton candy sunsets in South Dakota with her two little boys, a mischievous kitten and a lovable dog.